J 359.9 G

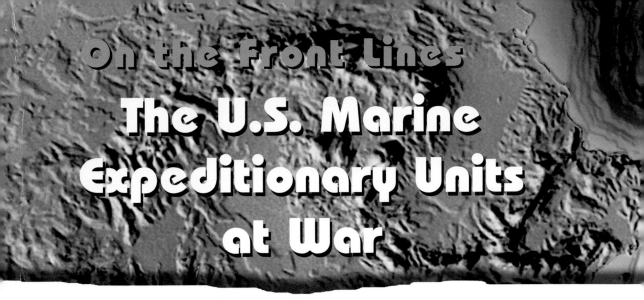

On the Front Lines

The U.S. Marine Expeditionary Units at War

by Michael and Gladys Green

Consultant:
Capt. Arnaldo L. Colón, USMC

CAPSTONE
HIGH-INTEREST
BOOKS
an imprint of Capstone Press
Mankato, Minnesota

Capstone High-Interest Books are published by Capstone Press
151 Good Counsel Drive, P.O. Box 669, Mankato, Minnesota 56002
http://www.capstone-press.com

Library of Congress Cataloging-in-Publication Data
Green, Michael, 1952–
    The U.S. Marine Expeditionary Units at war/by Michael and Gladys Green.
    p. cm.—(On the front lines)
    Includes bibliographical references and index.
    Contents: Marine Expeditionary Units (SOC)—MEU (SOC)
History—Recent conflicts—Today's MEU (SOC).
    ISBN 0-7368-2157-0 (hardcover)
    1. United States. Marine Corps—Juvenile literature. 2. Special forces
(Military science)—United States—Juvenile literature. [1.United States. Marine
Corps. 2. Special forces (Military science)]
I. Green, Gladys, 1954– II. Title. III. Series.

VE23.G7397 2004
359.9'6352'0973—dc21   2002155042

Summary: Provides an overview of the U.S. Marine Expeditionary Units (Special
    Operations Capable), its missions, members, history, recent conflicts, and
    modern equipment.

Editorial Credits
James Anderson, editor; Steve Christensen, series designer; Jason Knudson, book
    designer; Jo Miller, photo researcher; Karen Risch, product planning editor

Photo Credits
Corbis/AFP, 4–5, 14, 20; Bettmann, 13; Reuters New Media Inc., 24–25
Corporal Rathal F. Wills, Combat Photographer, 26th MEU (SOC), cover
Defense Visual Information Center, 6, 8, 16–17, 23, 27
Lockheed Martin Aeronautics Company, 28
Photri-Microstock, 10–11

1 2 3 4 5 6 08 07 06 05 04 03

Table of Contents

CHAPTER 1

Learn about:

- **MEU groups**

- **Amphibious Operations**

- **Direct Action missions**

MEU (SOC) members protected an airport during Operation Enduring Freedom.

MEU (SOC)

In December 2001, a Marine from the 15th Marine Expeditionary Unit (Special Operations Capable) patrols an airport in Afghanistan. He carries a M16A2 rifle with a grenade launcher. His face is covered to protect his skin from blowing sand.

The Marine is part of Operation Enduring Freedom. His job is to keep the airport safe from an enemy terrorist group.

MEU (SOC)

A Marine Expeditionary Unit (MEU) is a force of about 2,200 Marines and sailors. There are currently seven MEUs within the Marine Corps.

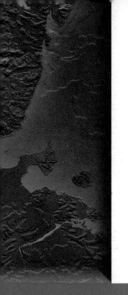

Each MEU is divided into four groups. These groups are the Command Element (CE), the Ground Combat Element (GCE), the Aviation Combat Element (ACE), and the Combat Service Support Element (CSSE).

Marines of an MEU (SOC) travel in helicopters of the Aviation Combat Element, like the CH-46 Sea Knight.

The CE is an MEU's smallest group. More than 200 Marines and sailors serve in the CE. The CE is in charge of the other three groups and plans their missions. The CE includes anti-aircraft and reconnaissance units. These units shoot down enemy aircraft. They also explore enemy areas to gain information.

The GCE is the largest MEU group. 1,200 to 1,300 Marines may be in this group. About 900 are infantrymen. The remaining Marines drive tanks, trucks, and other vehicles. They also provide artillery support.

Nearly 500 Marines make up an ACE. The ACE flies four types of helicopters. These are the CH-46E Sea Knight, CH-53 Super Stallion, UH-1N Huey, and AH-1W SuperCobra. The SuperCobra is armed with machine guns and rockets. Each ACE also has six AV-8B Harriers, which it uses to conduct air raids.

A CSSE is made up of about 300 Marines. These groups send food, drinking water, and fuel to the other MEU groups.

Amphibious Operations take place on land and water.

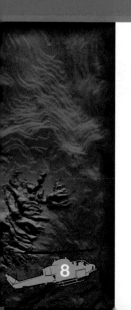

MEU (SOC) Missions

MEU (SOC)s perform many types of missions. Each mission falls into one of four categories. These are Amphibious Operations, Operations Other Than War, Supporting Operations, and Direct Action missions.

Amphibious Operations have always been the most important job of the Marines. These missions take place on land and water. On these missions, Marines may attack an enemy camp. They also may capture an enemy airport.

Operations Other Than War missions help people after a natural disaster. In a poor country, Marines help build roads, bridges, schools, and houses. These missions also include peacekeeping operations and riot control.

On Supporting Operations, the CSSE sends gear, food, and supplies. The supplies are sent to other MEU (SOC) groups while they are on missions. Supplies are also sent to countries in need around the world.

During Direct Action missions, MEU members may rescue Americans from an enemy country. Marines on Direct Action missions might stop ships and search them for people or illegal cargo.

CHAPTER 2

Learn about:

- **Fleet Marine Forces**

- **Marine Afloat Battalions**

- **Persian Gulf**

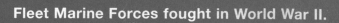
Fleet Marine Forces fought in World War II.

MEU (SOC) History

During World War I (1914–1918), Marines fought alongside U.S. Army troops. After the war, some Americans questioned the need for two land armies.

Marine Expeditionary Unit History

Marine leaders knew they were needed for more missions. Some Marines saw Japan as the next threat to the United States. Soon after World War I, Japanese forces began to build amphibious bases. They built them on many islands in the Pacific Ocean.

The Marines soon began training to move their equipment from Navy ships onto Japanese shores. These Marines joined a Marine Corps Expeditionary Force. In 1933, this group was renamed Fleet Marine Forces.

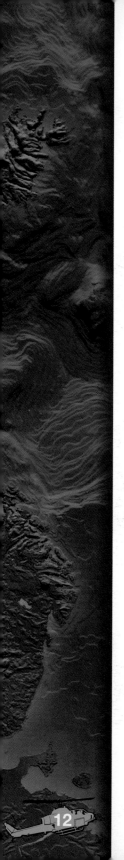

During World War II (1939–1945), the Fleet Marine Forces grew. They formed six groups of about 18,000 men. The Navy built hundreds of ships to carry these Marines to battle.

Postwar Reorganization

There were almost 460,000 Marines near the end of World War II. After the war, the number dropped to fewer than 200,000.

The Marine Corps then shared troops with part of the Navy. They formed Marine Afloat Battalions.

Name Changes

In the 1970s, the Marine Afloat Battalions were named Marine Amphibious Units (MAUs). In 1983, the Marine Corps changed the MAUs' name to the Marine Expeditionary Unit (MEU).

MEUs performed special operations missions. Marine leaders believed that future conflicts would involve small Marine units. Marines in special operations forces fight drug dealers, terrorists, and traditional armies.

Marines have been sent on amphibious missions for many years.

The U.S. Army, Navy, and Air Force each had formed small groups of highly trained men. The Marine Corps decided to train regular units in special operations. This would make them Special Operations Capable (SOC).

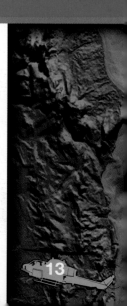

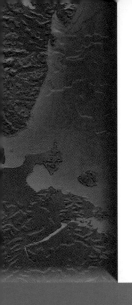

MEU (SOC) in Action

In 1985, the 26th MEU (SOC) became the first MEU to go to sea. The unit did not enter combat on its six-month cruise. The first unit to go into combat was the 22nd MEU (SOC).

MEU (SOC) Marines paint their faces with camouflage paint before some missions.

In 1989, the Iranian navy placed underwater mines in the Persian Gulf. The mines damaged a U.S. Navy ship.

The Iranian navy used several offshore oil platforms in the Persian Gulf as bases. The 22nd MEU (SOC) destroyed the oil platforms. Marine aircraft and Navy planes and ships helped the Marines on this mission. The aircraft sank or damaged many Iranian navy ships.

Marines have been involved in many conflicts. Their missions are often behind enemy lines. Some missions they have performed remain a military secret.

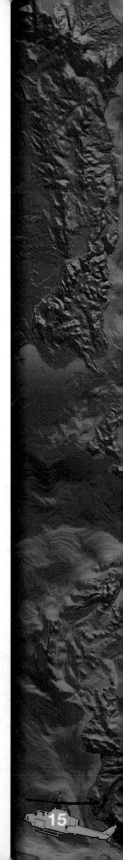

CHAPTER 3

Learn about:

■ A fake invasion

■ Somalia

■ Fight against
terrorism

MEU (SOC) units were a part of Operation
Desert Shield.

Recent Conflicts

In 1991, the country of Kuwait had been invaded by military forces from its neighboring country Iraq. U.S. military forces prepared to free the people of Kuwait.

Operation Desert Shield

More than 17,000 Marines were based on ships near Iraq. The 13th MEU (SOC) was part of this force. This unit practiced landing on beaches in Kuwait.

The Iraqi army believed that Marines would invade from the sea. Iraq stationed more than 80,000 troops along the beaches. The Iraqi troops waited for a Marine invasion that never came. U.S. forces invaded from land in the opposite direction.

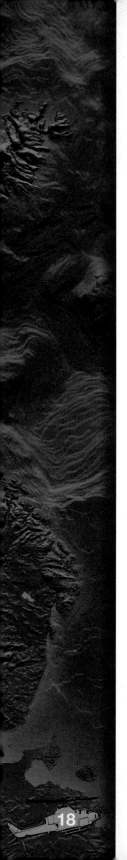

Operation Provide Comfort

In April 1991, the 24th MEU (SOC) took part in Operation Provide Comfort. They helped rescue more than 1 million starving and sick people in Iraq. The people had been attacked by the Iraqi army.

The unit also helped set up refugee camps. These camps were places where people who were fleeing Iraq could go for food and shelter. Operation Provide Comfort ended on July 24, 1991.

Other MEU (SOC) Operations

In 1992 and 1993, Marines took part in Operation Restore Hope. The U.S. military delivered food and medical supplies to the people of Somalia in Africa. Marines also helped repair the country's roads, schools, and hospitals.

In June 1995, the 24th MEU (SOC) helped rescue U.S. Air Force fighter pilot Captain Scott O'Grady. His plane had been shot down over the country of Bosnia-Herzegovina. The Marines, with the help of other U.S. troops, used a CH-46 Sea Knight helicopter to rescue O'Grady.

Important Dates

1933—Fleet Marine Forces formed.

1939—World War II begins.

1983—Marine Amphibious Units are named Marine Expeditionary Units.

1985—26th MEU (SOC) goes out to sea.

1989—22nd MEU (SOC) sees combat in the Persian Gulf.

1991—13th MEU (SOC) stages a fake invasion on Iraqi-controlled beaches.

1992—Operation Restore Hope begins.

1995—24th MEU (SOC) rescues U.S. Air Force fighter pilot Captain Scott O'Grady.

2001—Terrorists attack New York and Washington, D.C., on September 11. The 15th and 26th MEU (SOC)s land in Afghanistan on November 25.

2002—The 26th MEU (SOC) is attacked by terrorists while guarding an airport in Afghanistan. Pilots and flight crews from the 13th MEU (SOC) work with U.S. Army troops to capture terrorists.

2003—U.S. and Allied forces take part in Operation Iraqi Freedom.

Marines searched for terrorists in Operation Enduring Freedom.

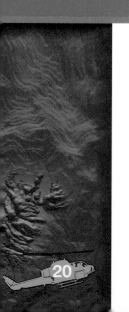

Operation Enduring Freedom

U.S. Marines landed in Afghanistan by helicopter and by plane on November 25, 2001. The Marines were from the 15th and 26th MEU (SOC)s.

The Marines' mission was to attack or capture terrorists hiding in Afghanistan. The terrorists belonged to an organization known as al-Qaida. They were being protected by a military group called the Taliban.

On January 10, 2002, Taliban troops attacked Marines from the 26th MEU (SOC). The Marines were guarding an airport in Afghanistan. In a fierce battle, the Marines defeated the enemy troops.

In March 2002, U.S. helicopters and planes attacked Taliban forces hiding in the mountains of Afghanistan. The 13th MEU (SOC) Marine pilots and flight crews worked with U.S. Army troops. Many terrorists were captured.

Operation Iraqi Freedom

MEU (SOC) forces took part in missions during Operation Iraqi Freedom. During this operation, MEU (SOC) forces were some of the first ground troops to arrive in Iraq. Marines were stationed on the front lines of many battles. Some MEU (SOC) missions in Iraq remain a military secret.

SuperCobra

Function:	Attack helicopter
First Deployed:	1986
Speed:	170 miles (274 kilometers) per hour
Range:	395 miles (636 kilometers)
Weight:	14,750 pounds (6,690 kilograms)

About 147 SuperCobras are in Marine service. The SuperCobra has several jobs. One job of the SuperCobra is to protect other Marine helicopters and Marines on the ground.

Another job is to attack enemy vehicles. During Operation Desert Storm, SuperCobras destroyed 104 Iraqi trucks and 97 Iraqi tanks.

The Marine Corps' SuperCobra has two engines. This is important for helicopters in case one engine fails.

Two people pilot the SuperCobra. The copilot sits in the front. The pilot sits behind him.

CHAPTER 4

Learn about:

■ Bases

■ F-35B Strike Fighter

■ Future

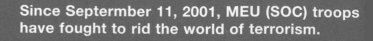

Since Septermber 11, 2001, MEU (SOC) troops have fought to rid the world of terrorism.

Today's MEU (SOC)

All Marines are trained to respond quickly to emergencies. MEU (SOC)s are the most flexible units in the Marine Corps. They are often the first to respond to a military situation.

Current Organization

The 11th, 13th, and 15th MEU (SOC) groups have their home base at Camp Pendleton, California. The 22nd, 24th, and 26th are based at Camp Lejeune, North Carolina. The 31st MEU (SOC) is based in Okinawa, Japan.

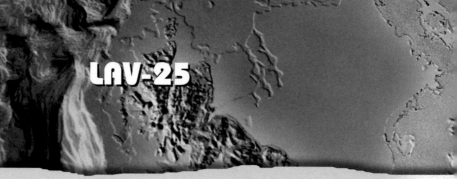

LAV-25

Function:	Armored Reconnaissance Vehicle
Date Deployed:	1983
Speed:	62 miles (100 kilometers) per hour
Range:	430 miles (692 kilometers)
Weight:	15 tons (13.6 metric tons)

The full name for the LAV-25 is the Light Armored Vehicle-25. General Motors of Canada built almost 800 models of this vehicle for the U.S. Marine Corps.

The LAV-25 has a three-person crew. The crew includes the vehicle commander, the gunner, and the driver. The vehicle has room in its rear for six more Marines. The LAV-25 can be carried inside cargo planes. It can also be carried under large helicopters.

The LAV-25 can travel in calm inland water such as lakes and rivers. Marines do not use the LAV-25 in the ocean. In the water, it has a top speed of 6 miles (9.7 kilometers) per hour.

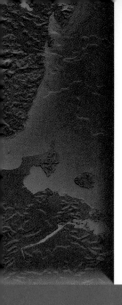

New Jet Plane

The Marines hope to replace older weapons and equipment. New equipment will help the Marines better perform their missions.

The F-35B will be the next Marine jet in service.

The Marines now use the jet-powered AV-8B Harrier II ground attack plane. It supports MEU (SOC) operations. The AV-8B Harrier II can land and take off like a helicopter.

The Marines are counting on the F-35B Strike Fighter to replace the AV-8B Harrier II. Each new F-35B costs about $30 million. The first new F-35B may enter service by 2011.

Future MEO (SOC) Operations

Terrorism has become common in today's world. MEU (SOC) forces train and prepare to travel throughout the world to protect U.S. interests. MEU (SOC) forces may storm a beach as a part of an amphibious operation. Other times, they might drop from a helicopter during a top-secret mission.

Whenever they are needed, the MEU (SOC)s are a valuable military force. The MEU (SOC)s will continue to perform important missions for the U.S. military.

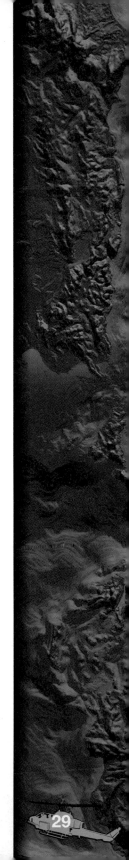

Words to Know

amphibious (am-FIB-ee-uhss)—able to operate both on land and in water

corps (KOR)—a group of military officers and enlisted members

expeditionary (ek-spuh-DIH-shuh-nair-ee)—trips or missions with a purpose, such as watching enemy troops or attacking enemy airports

mission (MISH-uhn)—a military task

operation (op-uh-RAY-shuhn)—an event that has been carefully planned and involves a group or groups of people

reconnaissance (ree-CAH-nuh-suhns)—exploring enemy areas to gain information

refugee (REF-yuh-jee)—a person who is forced to leave his or her home because of war or natural disaster; Marines may set up refugee camps in troubled areas.

terrorist (TER-ur-ist)—someone who uses violence or threats to get what they want from a group of people or government; terrorists often act for political or religious reasons.

To Learn More

Aaseng, Nathan. *The Marine Corps in Action.* U.S. Military Branches and Careers. Berkeley Heights, N.J.: Enslow Publishers, 2001.

Hopkins, Ellen. *U. S. Special Operations Forces.* U.S. Armed Forces. Chicago: Heinemann Library, 2003.

Voeller, Edward A. *U.S. Marine Corps Special Forces: Recon Marines.* Warfare and Weapons. Mankato, Minn.: Capstone Press, 2000.

Useful Addresses

Marine Corps Division of Public Affairs
Headquarters Marine Corps
The Pentagon, Room SE-774
Washington, DC 20380-1775

Marine Corps Historical Center
1254 Charles Morris Street SE
Washington Navy Yard, DC 20374-5040

Internet Sites

Do you want to find out more about Marine Expeditionary Units?
Let FactHound, our fact-finding hound dog, do the research for you.

Here's how:

1) Visit *http://www.facthound.com*
2) Type in the **Book ID** number: **0736821570**
3) Click on **FETCH IT**.

FactHound will fetch Internet sites picked by our editors just for you!

Index